Alison Hawes
Illustrated by Charlotte Combe

A Harcourt Achieve Imprint

www.Rigby.com
1-800-531-5015

"I am going away," said Snake.

Snake's House

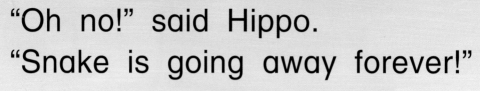

"Oh no!" said Hippo.
"Snake is going away forever!"

4

Snake's House

5

"Oh no!" said Giraffe.
"Snake is going away forever!"

6

Snake's House

7

"Oh no!" said Monkey.
"Snake is going away forever!"

Snake's House

9

"Don't go away forever, Snake!" said Monkey.

Snake's House

"I'm not going away forever," said Snake.

Snake's House

13

"I'm going away on vacation!"

Florida

Taxi

15